ESSENTIAL SPORTS

rugby

Andy Smith

Heinemann
LIBRARY

Contents

The 1999 World Cup final between Australia and France was played in front of 72,500 spectators at the Millennium Stadium in Cardiff.

ESSENTIAL SPORTS

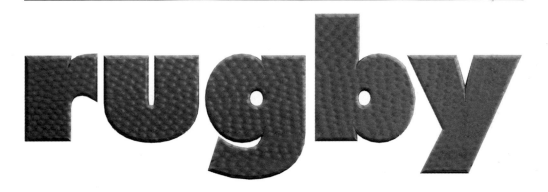

rugby

ESSENTIAL SPORTS – RUGBY
was produced by

David West 👥 **Children's Books**

7 Princeton Court
55 Felsham Road
London SW15 1AZ

Designer: Gary Jeffrey
Editor: James Pickering
Picture Research: Carlotta Cooper

First published in Great Britain by Heinemann
Library, Halley Court, Jordan Hill, Oxford
OX2 8EJ, part of Harcourt Education.
Heinemann is a registered trademark
of Harcourt Education Ltd.

07 06 05 04 03
10 9 8 7 6 5 4 3 2 1

ISBN 0 431 17370 2 (HB)
ISBN 0 431 17377 X (PB)

British Library Cataloguing in Publication Data

Smith, Andy
Rugby. - (Essential Sports)
1. Rugby football - Juvenile literature
I. Title
796.3'33

Printed and bound in Italy

PHOTO CREDITS :
Abbreviations: t-top, m-middle, b-bottom, r-right,
l-left, c-centre.

Front cover - David Rogers, Getty Images. Pages 3,
26b (Warren Little), 4, 9bl, 11, 13l, 16t, 19b, 20,
22bl, 23t, 24br, 28tr, 29 all, 30 both (David
Rogers), 4-5, 17b, 25t (Ben Radford), 5, 8tr (Mark
Thompson), 7b (Sean Garnsworthy), 8l, 23br (Nick
Laham), 8br (Ian Walton), 10, 16b (Mike Finn-
Kelcey), 12t (Stu Forster), 12bl (Peter Norton),
12br, 24bl (Jamie McDonald), 14r (Chris
McGrath), 14l, 27t (Alex Livesey), 14-15, 21t, 28tl
(Phil Cole), 15t, 22br, 23bl, 24t (Mike Hewitt),
15m (Gary M. Prior), 15b (Shaun Botterill), 17t
(Laurence Griffiths), 18t (Pascal Rondeau), 18b
(Michael Cooper), 19t (Russell Cheyne), 21b
(David Cannon), 22t (Ross Kinnaird), 25b (Darren
England), 26t (Steve Bardens), 26m (Darren Little),
27b (Adam Pretty), 28bl (Clive Mason), 28br (Scott
Barbour), 6 all, 9t - Getty Images. 8tl, 9br - Corbis
Images.

*An explanation of difficult words can be
found in the glossary on page 31.*

England's Nicola Crawford breaks through France's defence at Twickenham during the 2002 Women's Six Nations Tournament.

Introduction

Rugby Union has grown in popularity in recent years, especially since it became 'open' in 1995 when professionalism was first allowed. Huge TV audiences watch internationals and Super 12 games live from the other side of the world.

Even the Varsity match between Oxford and Cambridge at Twickenham attracts a vast crowd, many of whom have no connection with either university. Many youngsters learn the skills of this complicated game at an early age. Most clubs now run mini rugby sections for under-10s, who want to play like their heroes, such as the dashing Ireland centre Brian O'Driscoll, England's cool outside-half Jonny Wilkinson or the powerful Wales no. 8 Scott Quinnell. Rugby continues to grow, with 20 nations involved in the final stages of the 2003 World Cup.

Dafydd Jones of Wales is highest in the line-out in the 2003 RBS Six Nations match against Ireland in Cardiff.

History of the game

It is said that the game began when a cheeky Rugby schoolboy picked up the ball during a game of football and ran with it.

Like football, rugby evolved from the free-for-all games that had been played since the Middle Ages.

'A FINE DISREGARD'

On the wall of the Close at Rugby School in central England, a plaque commemorates 'the exploit of William Webb Ellis, who, with a fine disregard for the rules of football as played in his time, first took the ball in his arms and ran with it, thus originating the distinctive feature of the Rugby game. AD 1823'. Most experts now agree that Webb Ellis probably had very little to do with the origins of rugby, and that a form of the game was being played almost 2,000 years before in Roman times – 'harpastum'. In the Middle Ages, many villages in England played day-long games with vast numbers on each side attempting to carry the ball through the 'goal' of the opposition.

William Webb Ellis

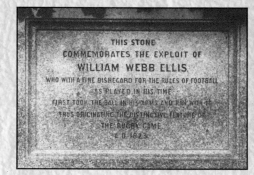

THIS STONE COMMEMORATES THE EXPLOIT OF WILLIAM WEBB ELLIS WHO WITH A FINE DISREGARD FOR THE RULES OF FOOTBALL AS PLAYED IN HIS TIME FIRST TOOK THE BALL IN HIS ARMS AND RAN WITH IT THUS ORIGINATING THE DISTINCTIVE FEATURE OF THE RUGBY GAME A.D 1823

The plaque at Rugby School, marking Webb Ellis's unorthodox action

Rugby School gave its name to the sport William Webb Ellis is said to have started. Writers have since disputed the part Webb Ellis played in the beginnings of Rugby Union, claiming that running with the ball was not allowed at the school until 15 years later.

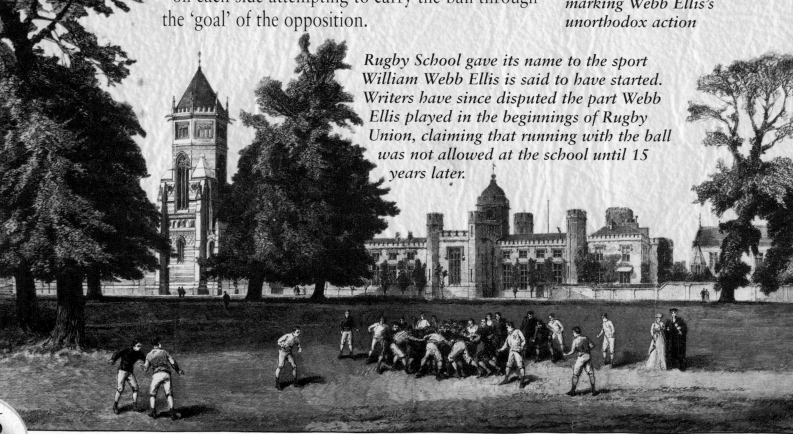

EVOLUTION AND A SPLIT

The Rugby Football Union, formed in 1871, drew up the first set of laws. Later that year, the first international, between Scotland and England was played, with 20 players on each side. This remained common in England until fifteens (XVs) were introduced at the Oxford-Cambridge match of 1875 and into international rugby in 1877. Clubs were founded – there were over 20 in the London area alone by 1864 – and the game became popular in the north. In 1895, 21 northern clubs, annoyed that they were not allowed to pay their players, broke away from the RFU to form the Northern Union (later the Rugby Football League).

At Harrow School in the 1920s, they were playing according to Rugby Football Union laws originally introduced in 1871.

THE MODERN GAME

By the end of the 19th century, rugby was being played all over the British Isles, in Australia, South Africa, New Zealand, France and Argentina. The first overseas team to tour England was the New Zealand Maoris in 1888. The Five Nations Championship, between England, France, Ireland, Scotland and Wales, came into its own after World War II, Italy joining in 2000. The Tri Nations Championship featuring Australia, South Africa and New Zealand was not established until 1996.

Ireland's Keith Wood with the ball for the British and Irish Lions in the second Test match against Australia in 2001

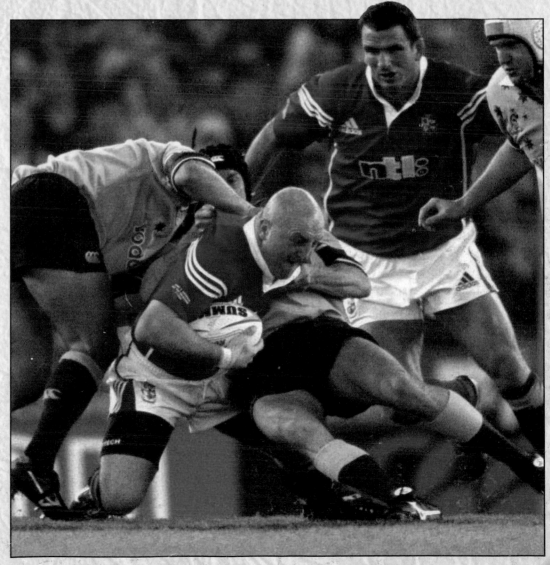

Kit

As the players have become fitter and stronger, and the game faster, the need for better kit has increased.

Rugby kit, especially designed for the modern game, has also become a fashion item. It's not unusual to see a Wallabies shirt worn in the high street.

Protective kit is available for youngsters playing mini rugby. It is always a good idea for head protection to be worn.

GUM SHIELD
This simple device is designed to protect the mouth and front teeth.

CLOTHING AND PROTECTION

Rugby union is an intense, very physical, contact game. Some players have always worn a form of head protection – a photograph taken in 1906 shows two forwards apparently in bathing hats! Scrum caps, bands of leather that passed over the head, were worn 50 years ago, but current head gear covers the ears and whole head apart from the face. Soft shoulder pads cover the shoulder and collarbone.

BOOTS
Players used to wear heavy leather boots which only became heavier in damp, muddy conditions. Modern boots, made from a combination of leather and synthetic materials, are much lighter, don't absorb moisture and can take a variety of studs.

KIT HISTORY

Players of the early types of rugby wore shirts with long sleeves and collars, long pants, boots covering the ankles and often caps. Sometimes the caps were the only way of differentiating between players on each side. By the start of the 20th century, the kit still covered most of the body, with shorts stretching down below the knee. In fact, kit did not change much until the mid-1960s when the shorts were shorter and boots became lighter with screw-in studs. Studs now must not be longer than 1.8 cm. Wearing a single stud at the toe of the boot is not allowed.

Early rugby kit must have reduced, rather than increased, speed and mobility.

THE RUGBY BALL

Early 20th century balls were made of leather with a pig's bladder inside. The design had hardly changed since the 1850s. It became very heavy when wet.

It is not known when the rugby ball changed from being round to oval. Reports from Rugby School in the 1830s refer to the ball 'pointing towards the school or the island goal' – therefore it must have been oval. The oldest surviving rugby ball dates from 1851 and that is definitely oval, made of four pieces of cowhide stitched together. Today's ball is of synthetic material with four panels and no visible stitching.

Jonah Lomu leads the New Zealand All Blacks in the traditional haka (war dance) at the start of a match. They wear specially-made 'slippery' kit which is difficult for opponents to grip.

The modern ball weighs between 400 and 440 g when fully inflated, and because it is waterproof, that weight does not change in damp conditions.

Pitch and positions

The game has been 15-a-side since 1875, and the positions have remained largely unchanged since Welsh clubs devised a system with seven men behind the scrum in 1878.

THE PITCH

The basic field of play is bounded by, but does not include, the goal-lines, the touch lines and the in-goal area (the area between the dead ball line and the goal-line). In Britain, the game is usually played on a natural grass surface which, because of the climate, tends to produce soft and often wet conditions. In hotter parts of the world, the fields are drier and harder. If grass pitches are not available, the surface may be of sand or clay.

In-goal area

Maximum length 100 m

Half way line

10-metre line

22-metre line

22 m

5-metre line

Maximum width 69 m

Goal-line

Dead ball line

Northampton Saints ready for the kick-off

KICK-OFF
The captain who wins the toss of a coin decides whether his or her side will kick off or which goal-line they will defend. The kick-off used to be taken from the centre of the half way line with the ball on a tee or a pile of sand. Now the kicker can use a drop-kick to start the game. All the kicker's side must be behind the ball when it is kicked, and the opposition must stand in their own half behind the 10-metre line. The ball must travel at least 10 metres into the opponents' half, not directly into touch, into the in-goal area, or over the dead ball line.

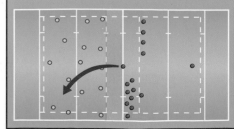

10

GOALPOSTS
For the purposes of a kick at goal, the two vertical posts are considered to extend indefinitely upwards.

6 m or more

3 m

5.6 m

THE OFFICIALS
The referee is in charge of the game, judging fair and unfair play, awarding yellow or red cards to book players and whistling to stop and start the game. Touch judges patrol the sidelines, indicating where the ball has gone out of play.

A touch judge runs the line in a European Cup semi-final between Castres and Munster in 2002.

5-metre indicators

Touch line

5-metre line

15 m indicators

Loosehead prop

Hooker

Tighthead prop

Lock

Lock

Flanker

Flanker

No. 8

1 **2** **3**

4 **5** **6** **7**

8

11 **9**

10 **12**

13

15 **14**

THE FORWALDS

THE BACKS

Winger

Scrum half

Fly half

Inside centre

Outside centre

Winger

Full back

How the players would line up before a scrum on the left side of the field (see page 16). Essentially, the forwards' job is to win the ball, the backs' task is to use it to score.

THE PLAYERS
When rugby became a 15-a-side game in the 1870s, the line-up consisted of nine forwards and six backs. In 1884, Frank Hancock of Cardiff successfully altered his club's line up to eight forwards and seven backs. At first the method did not work at international level, and it was only in 1894 that the system was accepted by all four British teams.

The rules

T he first set of rules, or laws, were drawn up in 1871. The laws have often been altered, but without drastically changing the game.

GAME BASICS

Rugby is a game of running, handling, passing and kicking an oval ball to score points. The ball may not be thrown or knocked forwards by any part of the body, except when it is kicked. Only a player in possession of the ball may be tackled by an opponent – knocked to the ground with the shoulder or gripped with the arms.

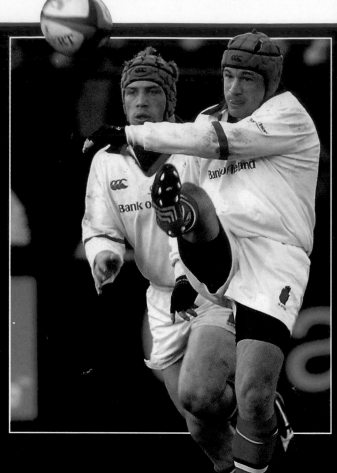

David Humphreys of Ulster and Ireland kicks a penalty against Cardiff at the Arms Park in the 2001 European Cup.

Gloucester flanker Andy Hazell scores a try for England A against Italy A at Northampton in 2003.

SCORING

5 **TRY** – worth five points, is scored when the ball is grounded in the opposition's in-goal area by a member of the attacking team. The ball must be placed on the ground with downward pressure or no try is scored.

2 **CONVERSION** – worth two points, is a kick taken in field and opposite the point at which the ball was grounded for the try. It must go over the bar and between the posts.

3 **PENALTY KICK** – worth three points, is a kick taken from the point at which an infringement occurs. Like a conversion, it must go over the bar and between the posts.

3 **DROP GOAL** – worth three points, is a kick from open play. The ball is bounced or dropped in front of the kicker immediately before being kicked over the bar and between the posts.

5 **PENALTY TRY** – worth five points, is awarded by the referee when the defending side commits an infringement preventing the attacking side scoring a try.

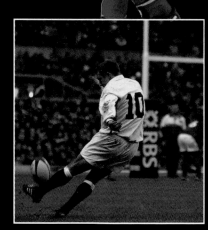

Jonny Wilkinson scored 77 points in the 2003 Six Nations Tournament.

RULE INFRINGEMENTS AND HALTS IN PLAY

⊘ FORWARD PASS – when a player unintentionally throws the ball forwards to a team mate. Referee's decision – a scrum at the point where the pass was made.

⊘ KNOCK ON – when a player unintentionally loses possession of the ball and it goes forwards. Referee's decision – a scrum at the point possession was lost. When a knock on is intentional to prevent the ball reaching an opposition player, the referee may award a penalty or a penalty try.

⊘ OFFSIDE IN OPEN PLAY – when a player attempts to play the ball or obstruct an opponent, and is in front of a team mate who has the ball or who last played the ball.

⊘ TACKLE – when a player with the ball is brought to the ground by one or more of the opposition.

⊘ LINE-OUT – the method of restarting the game after the ball has gone over the touchline (see page 17).

⊘ MARK – or fair catch, made when a player catches the ball from an opponent's kick when in his own in-goal or 22-metre area. Awarded with a free kick.

⊘ SCRUMMAGE – the method of restarting the game after a technical infringement, usually called 'scrum' (see page 16).

TECH TIPS – DROP KICK

This kick is used to restart the game after a score or after the ball has gone into touch in goal or over the dead ball line. It is also used to score a goal in open play or to convert a try.

1

2

3

1 *From the hands, drop the ball upright in front of the kicking foot.*

2 *As it hits the ground, kick the ball with the instep.*

3 *Follow through in the direction of the target.*

Leicester's flanker, All Black Josh Kronfeld, is penalised by referee Steve Lander.

THE BLOOD BIN

Any player who is bleeding or has an open wound is substituted until the bleeding stops and the wound is dressed. The injured player is referred to as being in the 'blood bin'. A player who is off the field for more than 15 minutes is regarded as having been permanently replaced.

No player is allowed to stay on the field with an open wound or when he or she is bleeding.

Forwards

Forwards are the eight players who make up the scrum. Scrummaging is a team effort requiring strength, coordination and concentration.

NO. 8

The best no. 8 forwards are excellent all round players and become involved in play all over the field. The no. 8 controls the scrum from the back, head between the inside legs of the two locks and binding tightly with the arms around the locks' outside hips. In a typical move, the ball is channelled through to the no. 8 who controls it with his feet before deciding the next move – either a heel for the scrum half, or a pick-up and charge around the scrum to find space.

Lawrence Dallaglio played no. 8 for England against Italy at Twickenham in 2003, frequently breaking through the defence, even with two men marking him.

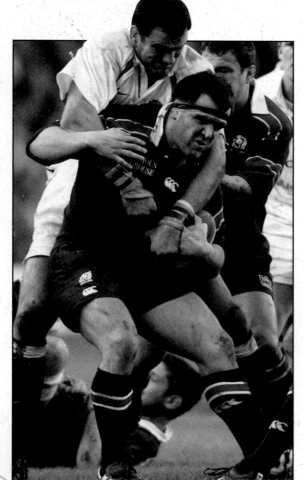

PROP

There are two props, one either side of the hooker. In the scrum, the left or loosehead prop ensures that the hooker has a clear view of the ball and enough height to enable him to rake the ball back with his foot. The right or tighthead prop binds with the hooker while pushing the opposing prop back.

Tom Smith, Scotland's loosehead prop can't escape the attentions of England lock Martin Johnson.

HOOKER

The hooker's primary task is to win the ball on his own team's put-in. With arms over or under the shoulders of his props, he binds the front row and strikes at the ball with his foot when it is passed into the scrum by the scrum half, to rake it back either through the middle of the scrum to the no. 8 or pushing it back between the left flanker and left lock. Good communication with the scrum half is vital.

Ireland hooker Keith Wood

LOCK

The two locks are in the second row, responsible for holding the scrum together and generating the power to propel the front row forwards. A lock's outside arm should be through the prop's legs with the hand gripping the prop's shirt above the shorts. The other arm should be around the other lock at armpit level. Locks are the usual targets for throwers at line-outs.

Italian lock Marco Bortolami wins the line-out ball against Ireland.

FLANKER

The flanker, or back row forward, should be a strong, mobile, athletic player. Flankers supply the power in the scrum to help the locks push the front row forwards. Flankers bind with the locks with their inside arm. On an opponent's put-in, the flanker is usually first to tackle.

French flanker Olivier Magne prevents All Black prop Joe McDonnell releasing the ball.

Forwards – set play

The first job of the forwards is to win the ball from the set pieces to set up their backs for an attack.

SCRUMS

Good scrummaging requires all eight forwards to work as a unit to drive forwards and destabilise the opponents' scrum. Each player has a particular role to make the scrum more effective. Good tight binding (using the arms to hold on to a team mate) is essential or the scrum will soon break up. The most important aspect of any scrum is to win the ball. Players must position their feet correctly to give them a firm base to push from, and to allow the ball passage from the hooker through the scrum to the back, either between the left flanker and the left lock, or through the legs of the left flanker to the no. 8. A strike against the head usually results in the ball travelling back through the legs of the right lock.

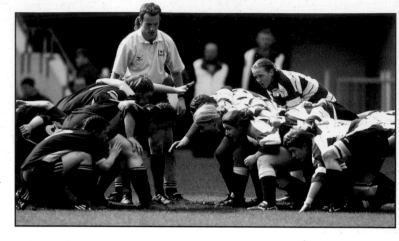

The referee's instructions to the two packs prior to a scrum are 'crouch, hold, engage'. He watches to make sure both teams bind correctly.

SCRUM FORMATION

No. 8
Flanker
Lock
Tighthead prop
Lock
Flanker
Hooker
Loosehead prop

The scrum half watches the passage of the ball as it is channelled back through the scrum. The pack stays down, driving to keep the opposition away from the ball.

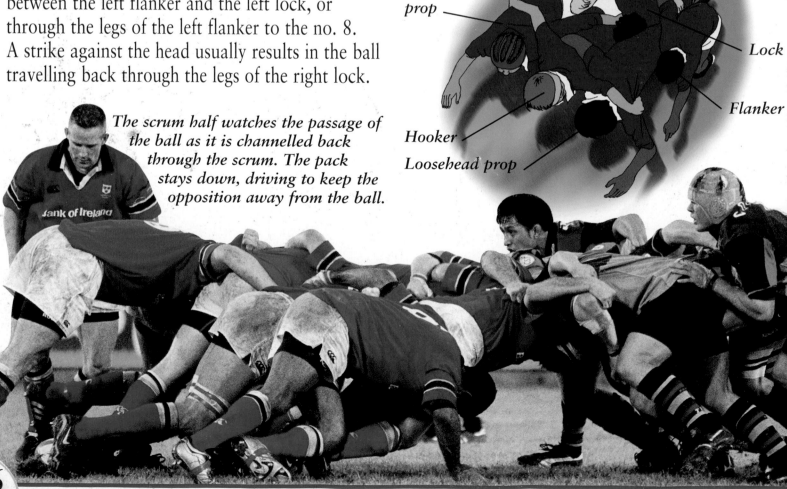

Bringing down the scrum is illegal and can be dangerous. Canada blame England at Twickenham in 1999.

Robert Sidoli, the Wales lock, supported by his team mates as he wins the ball at a line-out in the Six Nations match against Ireland in 2003.

LINE-OUTS

On average there are about 45 line-outs in a full match, so a team that dominates in the line-out often controls the game. The ball may be caught and held by the jumper, passed or deflected by the jumper to the scrum half or to another player in the line-out or thrown right over the top to a player not in the line-out.

TECH TIPS – TAKING THE LINE-OUT

Before taking the throw always decide who is the target in the line-out.

7 Flanker
6 No. 8
5 Flanker
4 Lock
3 Prop
2 Lock
1 Prop

5-m line

There must be a gap of 1 m between the two lines of players. The thrower cannot feint to throw the ball in, and the throw in must be straight. A player jumping for the ball must not be lifted but he can be supported after he has jumped. Pushing or charging in the line-out is illegal.

Hooker

Forwards – open play

Mauls and rucks develop in open play as both sets of players attempt to gain or keep possession of the ball.

Scotland's Chris Gray and Damien Cronin are at the centre of this maul against France at the Parc des Princes in 1991. Scrum half Gary Armstrong waits for the ball to be freed up.

MAULS

A maul is formed when one or more players from each team are on their feet and close around another player who is carrying the ball. The team with most players in the maul supporting the ball carrier has the better chance of emerging with it still in their possession. Even though players in a maul may be facing backwards, the maul should move forwards. To defend a maul, the ball carrier should be put on the ground where he must release the ball.

Ireland's Connor McGuinness clears the ball as the maul collapses.

HOW A ROLLING MAUL WORKS

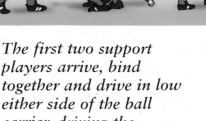

The ball carrier is tackled and held up. Team mates should try to arrive quickly on the scene in support.

The first two support players arrive, bind together and drive in low either side of the ball carrier, driving the opposition backwards.

The next support player drives in between the first two, support comes in on each side. The maul moves forwards with the ball or channels it back.

RUCKS

Unlike a maul, a ruck is formed when the ball is on the ground between players from each side, who are on their feet and in contact. A ruck is more likely to keep the move going forwards than a maul, but scrum halves prefer not to have to pick the ball up and pass from the ground. Support players coming into the ruck must drive in straight and from behind, not from the sides. When defending a ruck, the idea should be to wheel the opposition around to prevent them moving forwards. Stamping in a ruck is illegal.

England's forwards in a concerted effort to secure the ball, as the maul goes down against Ireland in a Five Nations International at Lansdowne Road in Dublin.

England's Martin Johnson tries to find the ball in a ruck against the New Zealand All Blacks at Twickenham in 1999.

TECH TIPS – HANDLING THE BALL ON THE GROUND

There are strict rules about when and how the ball can be taken from a player on the ground.

1

1 Legal – reaching over and grabbing the ball with both hands, but staying on your feet.

2

2 Illegal – grabbing the ball with one or both knees on the ground.

Half backs

South Africa's scrum half Joost Van der Westhuizen fires a pass to his stand-off Jannie de Beer in the 1999 World Cup match against Scotland.

Scrum halves and outside halves are the hub, the link between forwards and backs.

SCRUM HALF

A good scrum half has the full range of rugby skills at his disposal, but to be successful, he must know when and where to use them. He must be able to supply a variety of passes with either hand, and kick with either foot. Pace, stamina and agility are all useful attributes, but speed of thought and action – an ability to read a game and see openings, under constant pressure from the opposition – are essential. The top scrum halves, such as Australia's George Gregan and, in former times, Gareth Edwards of Wales, all exude an air of confidence and remain calm in all circumstances.

TECH TIPS – THE LONG PASS

A long pass at speed can be devastating.

1 If passing to the left, grab the ball with both hands but with the right in control. 2 Check your intended receiver as your weight shifts on to the left foot. 3 With a swing of the arm, release the ball, the pace and direction of the pass being controlled by the right hand. Also practise passing to the right.

Ball spins as it travels.

1   2   3

SKILL DRILL – LATERAL PASS

1 The player on the left passes to no. 8 who is approaching. 2 No 8 takes the ball on the move. 3 With a swing of the arms, he moves the ball on to his team mate on the right, keeping the ball moving and away from the opposition.

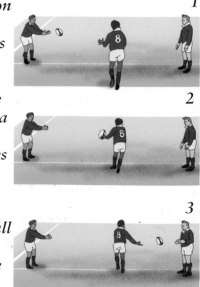

1
2
3

FLY HALF

Also known as the out half in Ireland and the stand-off in Wales, the fly half is often the most complete player on the team, with good handling, passing, running, kicking and tackling skills. In partnership with the scrum half, the fly half runs the midfield in a game and controls tactics. Using his range of skills, the fly half attempts to become unpredictable to the opposition, without confusing his own players. In defence, the fly half's job is to mark his opposite number at scrums and line-outs, trying to prevent him linking with his centres. At line-outs however, this could mean covering the centre, leaving a flanker, who is about ten metres closer, to deal with the opposition fly half.

Fly half Jonny Wilkinson kicks one of his four conversions in England's 40-5 victory over Italy at Twickenham in 2003.

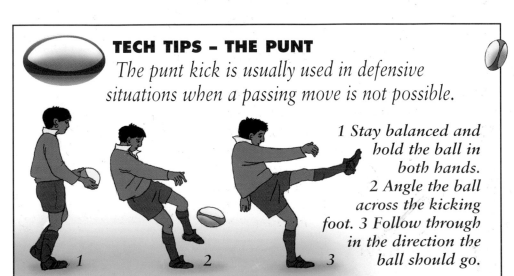

TECH TIPS – THE PUNT

The punt kick is usually used in defensive situations when a passing move is not possible.

*1 Stay balanced and hold the ball in both hands.
2 Angle the ball across the kicking foot. 3 Follow through in the direction the ball should go.*

1   2   3

Scotland's fly half Gregor Townsend tries to break away from England's Will Greenwood at Twickenham.

Three-quarter backs

The three-quarter line comprises two wingers and two centres, whose jobs are both offensive and defensive. There are few finer sights in rugby than a three-quarter line moving the ball smoothly between them at speed as they head for the opposition line.

One of the world's best outside centres, Ireland's Brian O'Driscoll, finds the Scotland defence, including wing Chris Paterson, in determined mood.

MULTI ROLE PLAYERS

Centres should have the energy to run and cover throughout the match in attack and defence, as well as excellent passing and receiving skills. This position requires the player to be an individual attacker on some occasions, a support player in attack on others, while the ability to tackle effectively is required in defence. The wingers are usually the fastest players on the team and the main try scorers, but they also have defensive responsibilities, in particular ensuring that opponents are not given the space to get around the back of the defence.

England winger Tony Underwood turns inside All Black Jonah Lomu in the 1995 World Cup semi-final at Cape Town.

Holding the ball when running with both hands gives players the option of passing to either side.

TECH TIPS – THE HAND-OFF AND THE DUMMY PASS

1

2

3

THE DUMMY PASS
1 As your opponent advances towards you, turn and make as if to pass the ball inside to your team mate. 2 The opponent moves to cover the pass, but you don't release it. 3 The opponent is wrong-footed and you have the chance to run on with the ball outside the defender and into space.

THE HAND-OFF
Ball away from the opponent, Tana Umaga of New Zealand prepares to hand off Bolla Conradie of South Africa.

SKILL DRILL – SWITCH PASS
The switch pass or 'scissor move' is used to change the direction of the attack. Timing of the pass is vital.

1

2

3

1 The ball carrier runs diagonally. Her team mate runs at a 90-degree angle. 2 The ball carrier passes the ball behind her to her team mate, switching the point of attack. 3 Because the receiver was behind the ball carrier, she cannot be penalised for crossing or blocking.

TACKLING
All three-quarters, wingers and centres need to be able to tackle. There are several ways of tackling, but the basic objectives should be to stop the ball carrier and to take possession of the ball. Tackles are best made from a balanced position to exert maximum force. The opponent should be grabbed firmly, the ball should be grasped if possible, especially close to the line where the opponents have a try scoring chance. Good tackles are rarely made with eyes closed.

Powerful tackling by England centre Will Carling forces New Zealand's full back Jeff Wilson to spill the ball.

Australian winger Ben Tune uses his strength to overcome an All Black tackle.

Full back

This exciting position is often the last line of defence and the first to start attacking moves.

DEFENDING

The keys to good defending are positional sense and the ability to anticipate the opposition's likely point of attack. When catching and fielding the ball, stay calm, even though there may be the risk of colliding with other players. A high ball is best left to the player going forwards towards it. Call to your team mates if that is you, and try not to let the ball bounce. When kicking the ball clear from inside the 22-metre line, aim to find touch. A full back's tackles often make the difference between an opponent scoring a try or not.

Full backs often tackle opponents bigger and stronger than themselves. Here, Wales's Kevin Morgan (1.77 m and 76 kg) meets Ireland's David Wallace (1.9 m and 95 kg).

Clearing the ball under pressure requires the full back to stay calm, or the kick could go anywhere!

ATTACKING

The full back can be part of an attack involving the backs (joining the line) or the initiator of those attacks. The full back can either break through the defence or provide support and create space for a team mate to do so. Some of the best opportunities to attack come when the opposition's kicks have been fielded by the full back.

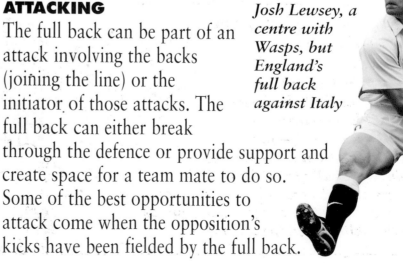

Josh Lewsey, a centre with Wasps, but England's full back against Italy

TECH TIPS – CATCHING THE HIGH BALL

England's Jason Robinson takes the ball against New Zealand in 2002.

1 Keep your eyes on the ball while moving forwards towards the ball. 2 If the opposition is close, the ball may have to be taken by the full back in the air. 3 Make sure both hands get to the ball. 4 Pull the ball into the body and decide whether to pass, kick or run.

MARKING THE BALL

A kick which arrives in the area between the 22-metre line and the goal-line without bouncing is caught cleanly by a defender, who calls 'mark' to the referee. If it is a fair catch, the referee awards the defender a free kick.

The area inside which defenders can call for a mark.

Mark! Richard Graham of the Queensland Reds makes a fair catch inside his own 22.

KICKING TO TOUCH – THE RULES
A Player inside his own 22 finds touch directly in the opponents' half. The line-out is taken from the point the ball crosses the touchline. B Player outside his own 22 kicks directly into touch – foul kick. The line-out is taken from the touchline, level with where the ball was kicked. C Player outside his own 22 kicks the ball into touch on the bounce – legal. The line-out is taken from the point where the ball crossed the touchline.

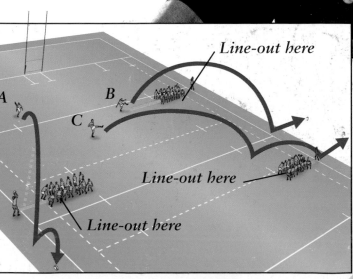

22-m line

A   B

C

Line-out here

Line-out here

Line-out here

Rugby variations

Various forms of rugby have developed over the years to enable those who are not big and powerful to enjoy the game.

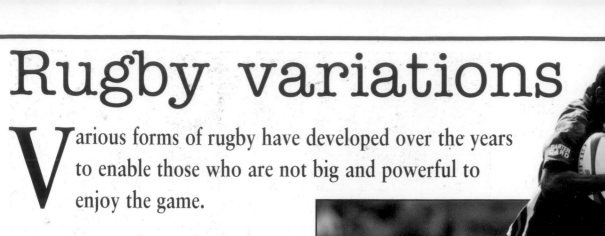

THE WORLD OF SEVENS

Seven-a-side rugby was invented in Scotland. Played on a full sized pitch, the seven players on each side are usually three forwards and four backs. Each half typically lasts seven minutes, but the latter stages of tournaments sometimes last longer, with one minute for half time. Various tournaments are staged throughout the world, with the game gaining great popularity through increased television coverage. The famous Hong Kong Sevens tournament is now part of the international series. Sevens first became a Commonwealth Games event at Kuala Lumpur in 1998.

Sevens rugby is very popular amongst female players. There was fierce competition between England and New Zealand in the 2003 Hong Kong Sevens tournament.

Paul Sackey of London Irish leaves three Northampton defenders floundering as he heads for the try line in the 2002 Middlesex Charity Sevens at Twickenham.

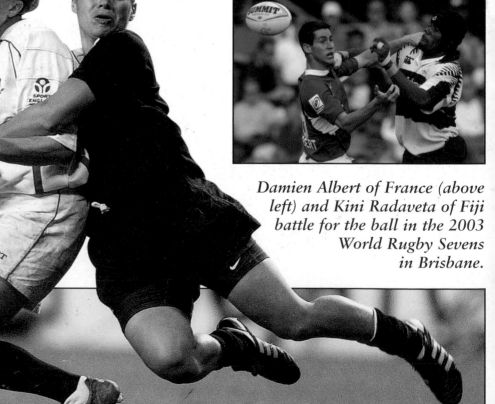

Damien Albert of France (above left) and Kini Radaveta of Fiji battle for the ball in the 2003 World Rugby Sevens in Brisbane.

MINI RUGBY

Revisions have been made to the full 15-a-side game so that even children below the age of seven can play. Pitch sizes are generally smaller, and matches shorter – under-sevens play two halves of ten minutes each, while under-twelves 'midi rugby' has two halves of 20 minutes each. Tackling is not allowed until the under-nine group. At earlier stages, opponents touch the ball carrier with two hands below the waist, and he or she must pass the ball within three strides.

Mini rugby at Rosslyn Park in London, one of the clubs where Rugby Union first developed.

Rugby League – Aussie style. Brad Fittler of the Sydney Roosters on the charge against the Cronulla Sharks.

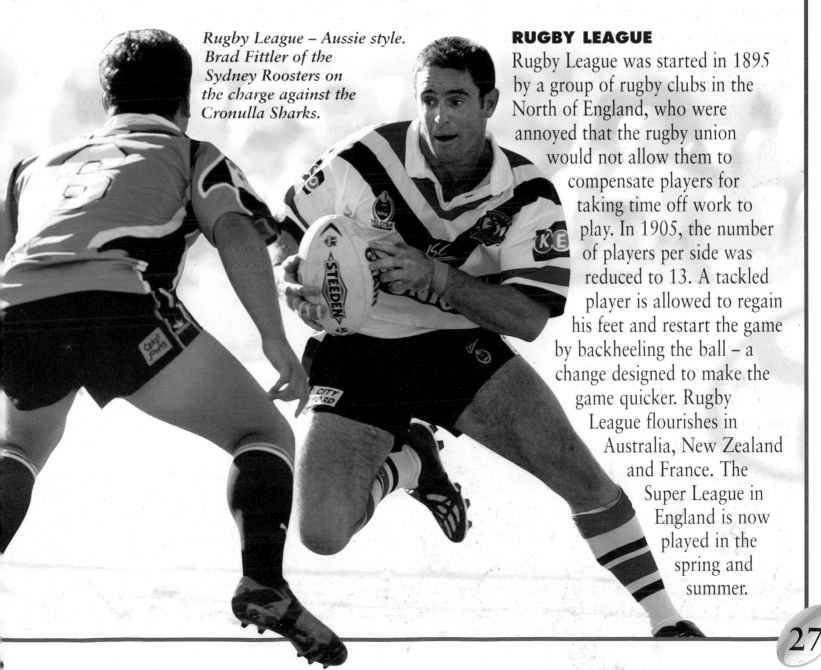

RUGBY LEAGUE

Rugby League was started in 1895 by a group of rugby clubs in the North of England, who were annoyed that the rugby union would not allow them to compensate players for taking time off work to play. In 1905, the number of players per side was reduced to 13. A tackled player is allowed to regain his feet and restart the game by backheeling the ball – a change designed to make the game quicker. Rugby League flourishes in Australia, New Zealand and France. The Super League in England is now played in the spring and summer.

World of rugby

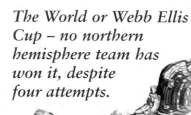

R ugby is played in over 100 countries with 94 national unions affiliated to the International Rugby Board.

Argentina played England in Buenos Aires in June 2002. England won the match 26-18.

England captain Martin Johnson lifts the Six Nations Trophy after winning the first Grand Slam (beating the five other teams) in the professional era.

INTERNATIONAL TOURNAMENTS

Of all the international tournaments, the World Cup is the most important and prestigious. It was first played for in 1987 in Australia and New Zealand. Other notable international tournaments include the Six Nations, featuring England, France, Ireland, Italy, Scotland and Wales, and the Tri Nations tournament between Australia, New Zealand and South Africa. In 2002, New Zealand beat England in the final of the Women's Rugby World Cup in Barcelona.

The World or Webb Ellis Cup – no northern hemisphere team has won it, despite four attempts.

THE BARBARIANS

This is the most exclusive rugby club in the world. It was formed in 1890 at a dinner in Bradford when a group of rugby officials led by W. P. Carpmael decided to take a team on a tour of the north of England. In 1947, the Barbarians took on the Australians at the end of their tour. The Barbarians versus the tourists is a highlight of the fixture list each year.

Kieran Roche (with the ball) and Josh Kronfeld in Barbarians colours against Wales at the Millennium Stadium in May 2002. The Barbarians won 40-25.

This map pinpoints the major rugby playing nations of the world, the 20 countries which qualified to take part in the 2003 World Cup in Australia.

1 Australia	11 England
2 Argentina	12 South Africa
3 Ireland	13 Georgia
4 Romania	14 Samoa
5 Namibia	15 Uruguay
6 France	16 New Zealand
7 Fiji	17 Wales
8 USA	18 Canada
9 Japan	19 Tonga
10 Scotland	20 Italy

Northern hemisphere team

Southern hemisphere team

Australia won the Tri Nations for the second year running in 2001, after which captain John Eales retired.

Women's rugby is one of the world's fastest growing sports. England, New Zealand and France are the top international sides. England won the 2003 Six Nations title after they came second in 2002, the year they beat Wales 40-0 at Old Deer Park.

TOURING TEAMS

Teams from Australia and New Zealand have been touring each other's countries since 1875 but a British team did not tour Australia and New Zealand until 1888. The first overseas team to visit Britain was the New Zealand Maoris later that year when they played a total of 74 matches! Rosslyn Park were the first British club side to play in France in 1893. The first team to be called the British Lions went to South Africa in 1924. In 2001, the British and Irish Lions were beaten in Australia, when the home side won a series against them for the first time.

Australia on their way to victory against the Lions in Sydney. Here, Australian wing Andrew Walker is tackled by Jason Robinson.

Fitness & training

To be successful in rugby, players must have the right attitude to fitness and training. Without it, there is no point in preparing for a match.

GENERAL FITNESS

Rugby requires that a player has stamina, speed, strength and suppleness. A player who is fit is less prone to injury and reacts more quickly on the field than an unfit player. Individual players should develop a fitness regime to suit the requirements of their position. So, a winger will need speed and endurance training more than, say, a prop. All players benefit from training that helps suppleness (such as stretching exercises) or builds strength (press-ups and pull-ups).

Start

Walk
Sprint
Stride

WINDERS
A winder is two lengths of the rugby pitch – younger players should cut the distance involved in this exercise, designed to improve stamina. Aim to increase the number of winders completed each session. Use the walk as the recovery period and remember to warm up and cool down properly even for training sessions. Drink water before and during training sessions.

TECH TIPS – TOUGHENING UP
Professional players use a variety of techniques to improve fitness and performance. Scrummage machines are now common at training sessions.

The Irish pack practise on a scrum machine during training at the Terenure Club in Dublin. Perfecting scrummaging techniques is essential, as research has shown that most games contain an average of 30 scrums, over 90 per cent of them lasting 20 seconds or more.

The England squad work with tackle bags on their training ground prior to the Six Nations match against Ireland, 2003.

Glossary

ALL BLACKS national team of New Zealand

BACKS players numbered 9 to 15

CONVERSION kick at goal after a try is scored. Worth two points if successful.

DROP GOAL kick at goal from open play. The ball must hit the ground before it is kicked. Worth three points if successful.

FLANKER either of the two forwards wearing number 6 or 7 (also known as wing forwards)

FLY HALF number 10, who normally receives the ball from the scrum half. Also known as out half in Ireland, stand off in Wales and first five-eighth in New Zealand.

FORWARD PASS illegal pass to a player ahead of the ball

FORWARDS players numbered 1 to 8, involved in scrums, line-outs, rucks and mauls

FRONT ROW collective name for the two props and the hooker, numbers 1, 2 and 3

INSIDE CENTRE back wearing number 12, also known as second five-eighth in New Zealand

KNOCK ON losing, dropping or knocking the ball forwards from a player's hand

LINE-OUT method of restarting play from the sidelines after the ball has gone into touch.

LOCK players numbered 4 and 5, usually the tallest players in the team, and targets for line-out throws

LOOSEHEAD number 1 prop in the scrum, named because his or her head is outside the opposition's tighthead prop's shoulders.

Further information

International Rugby Board
Huguenot House,
35/38 St Stephen's Green,
Dublin 2,
Ireland

Rugby Football Union
Rugby Road,
Twickenham,
Middlesex,
TW1 1DS

Irish RFU
Lansdowne Road,
Ballsbridge,
Dublin 4

Scottish Rugby Union
Murrayfield,
Edinburgh,
EH12 5PJ

Welsh Rugby Union
Custom House Street,
Cardiff,
CF10 1RF

Ulster Rugby
85 Ravenhill Park,
Belfast,
BT6 0DG

Australian Rugby Union
PO Box 188,
North Sydney,
NSW 2060

New Zealand RFU
1 Hinemoa Street,
Centrepoint,
PO Box 2172,
Wellington

South Africa RFU
Boundary Road,
PO Box 99,
Newlands,
Cape Town 7725

European Rugby Cup
Huguenot House,
35/38 St Stephen's Green,
Dublin 2,
Ireland

Index